Simply Diabetic Cookbook

GW01057526

A Detailed Diabetic Diet Cookbook with Gorgeous Recipes for Live Better!

Teresa Hance

Table of Contents

consent from the Publisher. All additional right reserved.

The information in the following pages is broadly considered a truthful and accurate account of facts and as such, any inattention, use, or misuse of the information in question by the reader will render any resulting actions solely under their purview. There are no scenarios in which the publisher or the original author of this work can be in any fashion deemed liable for any hardship or damages that may befall them after undertaking information described herein.

Additionally, the information in the following pages is intended only for informational purposes and should thus be thought of as universal. As befitting its nature, it is presented without assurance regarding its prolonged validity or interim quality. Trademarks that are mentioned are done without written consent and can in no way be considered an endorsement from the trademark holder.

Introduction

Diabetes mellitus, commonly known just as diabetes, is a disease that affects our metabolism. The predominant characteristic of diabetes is an inability to create or utilize insulin, a hormone that moves sugar from our blood cells into the rest of our bodies' cells. This is crucial for us because we rely on that blood sugar to power our body and provide energy. High blood sugar, if left untreated, can lead to serious damage of our eyes, nerves, kidneys, and other major organs. There are two major types of diabetes, type 1 and type 2, with the latter being the most common of the two with over 90 percent of diabetics suffering from it (Centers for Disease Control and Prevention, 2019).

HOW DOES INSULIN WORK?

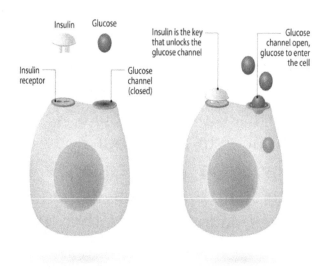

Type 1 diabetes is an autoimmune disease. In cases of type 1 diabetes, the immune system attacks cells in the pancreas responsible for insulin production. Although we are unsure what causes this reaction, many experts believe it is brought upon by a gene deficiency or by viral infections that may trigger the disease.

Type 1 Diabetes

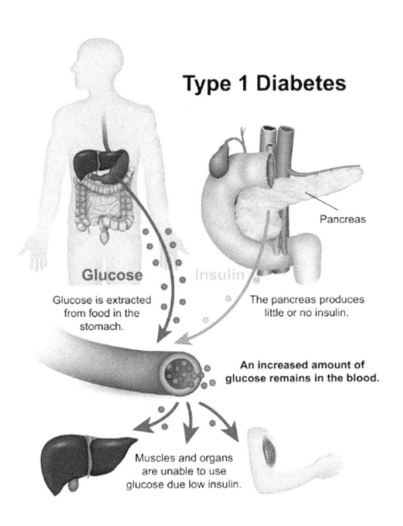

Pancreas

Glucose

Insulin

Glucose is extracted
from food in the
stomach.

The pancreas produces
little or no insulin.

**An increased amount of
glucose remains in the blood.**

Muscles and organs
are unable to use
glucose due low insulin.

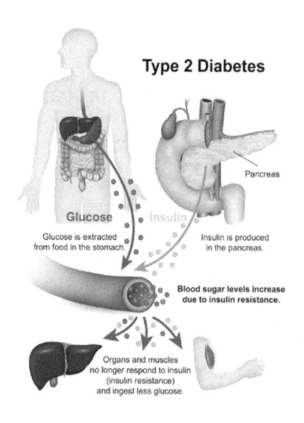

Type 2 Diabetes

Pancreas

Glucose

Insulin

Glucose is extracted from food in the stomach.

Insulin is produced in the pancreas.

Blood sugar levels increase due to insulin resistance.

Organs and muscles no longer respond to insulin (insulin resistance) and ingest less glucose.

Type 2 diabetes is a metabolic disorder, although research suggests it may warrant reclassification as an autoimmune disease as well. People who suffer from type 2 diabetes have a high resistance to insulin or an inability to produce enough insulin. Experts believe that type 2 diabetes is a result of a genetic predisposition in many people, which is further aggravated by obesity and other environmental triggers.

Diagnosis

Diabetes diagnosis has come incredibly far in the last few decades. Currently, there are two primary tests for diagnosing diabetes: the fasting plasma glucose (FPG) test and the hemoglobin A1c test.

The FPG test measures your blood sugar levels after an eight-hour fasting period; this helps to show if your body is processing glucose at a healthy rate.

The A1c test shows your blood sugar levels over the last three months. It does this by testing the amount of glucose being carried by the hemoglobin of your red blood cells. Hemoglobin has a lifespan of roughly three months; this allows us to test them to see how long they have been carrying their glucose for and how much they have.

Symptoms

In type 1 diabetes, the list of symptoms can be extensive with both serious and less obvious indicators. Below, I will list the most common symptoms as well as other potential complications of type 1 diabetes:

- **Excessive thirst:** Excessive thirst is one of the less noticeable indicators of type 1 diabetes. It is brought upon by high blood sugar (hyperglycemia).
- **Frequent urination:** Frequent urination is caused by your kidneys failing to process all of the glucose in your blood; this forces your body to attempt to flush out excess glucose through urinating.
- **Fatigue:** Fatigue in type 1 diabetes patients is caused by the body's inability to process glucose for energy.
- **Excessive hunger:** Those suffering from type 1 diabetes often have persistent hunger and increased appetites. This is because the body is desperate for glucose despite its inability to process it without insulin.
- **Cloudy or unclear vision:** Rapid fluctuations in blood sugar levels can lead to cloudy or blurred vision. Those suffering from untreated type 1 diabetes are unable to naturally control their blood sugar levels, making rapid fluctuations a very common occurrence.

- **Rapid weight loss:** Rapid weight loss is probably the most noticeable symptom of type 1 diabetes. As your body starves off glucose, it resorts to breaking down muscle and fat to sustain itself. This can lead to incredibly fast weight loss in type 1 diabetes cases.

SYMPTOMS OF TYPE 1 DIABETES

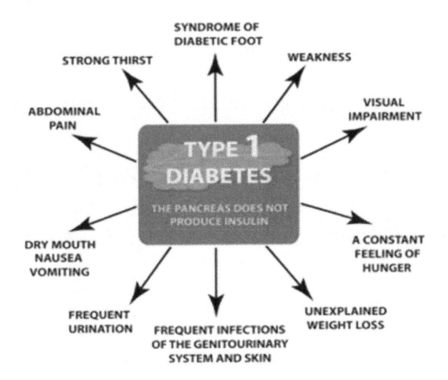

- **Ketoacidosis:** Ketoacidosis is a potentially deadly complication of untreated type 1 diabetes. In response to the lack of glucose being fed into your muscles and organs, your body starts breaking down your fat and muscle into an energy source called ketones, which can be burned without the need of insulin. Ketones are usually perfectly fine in normal amounts. But, when your body is starving, it may end up flooding itself with ketones in an attempt to fuel itself; the acidification of your blood that follows this influx of acid molecules may lead to more serious conditions, a coma, or death.

In cases of type 2 diabetes, the symptoms tend to be slower to develop, and they tend to be mild early on. Some early symptoms mimic type 1 diabetes and may include:

- **Excessive hunger:** Similar to type 1 diabetes, those of us with type 2 diabetes will feel constant hunger. Again, this is brought on by our bodies looking for fuel because of our inability to process glucose.

• **Fatigue and mental fog:** Depending on the severity of the insulin shortage in type 2 sufferers, they may feel physical fatigue and a mental fogginess during their average day.

• **Frequent urination:** Another symptom of both type 1 and 2 diabetes. Frequent urination is simply your body's way of attempting to rid itself of excess glucose.

• **Dry mouth and constant thirst:** It are unclear what causes dry mouth in diabetic sufferers, but it is tightly linked to high blood sugar levels. Constant thirst is brought on not only by a dry mouth but also by the dehydration that frequent urination causes.

SYMPTOMS OF TYPE 2 DIABETES

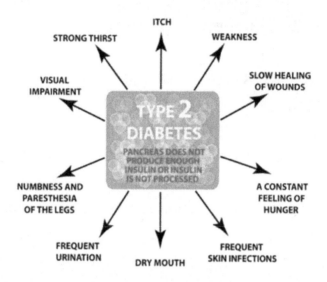

- **Itchy skin:** Itching of the skin, especially around the hands and feet, is a sign of polyneuropathy (diabetic nerve damage). As well as being a sign of potential nerve damage, itching can be a sign of high concentrations of cytokines circulating in your bloodstream; these are inflammatory molecules that can lead to itching. Cytokines are signaling proteins and hormonal regulators that are often released in high amounts before nerve damage.

As type 2 diabetes progresses and becomes more serious, the symptoms can become highly uncomfortable and dangerous. Some of these advanced symptoms include:

- **Slow healing of bruises, cuts, and abrasions:** Many people suffering from type 2 diabetes have impaired immune systems due to the lack of energy available to the body. As well as a lack of energy, many diabetics have slowed circulation brought upon by high blood glucose levels. Both of these factors lead to a much slower healing process and far greater risks of infection.
- **Yeast infections:** In women with type 2 diabetes, the chances of yeast infections are far higher than in non-diabetic women. This is due to high blood sugar levels and a lowered immune system response.
- **Neuropathy or numbness:** Long-term high blood sugar levels can lead to severe nerve damage in adults with diabetes. It is believed around 70 percent of people with type 2 diabetes have some form of neuropathy (Hoskins, 2020). Diabetic neuropathy is characterized by a numbness in the extremities, specifically around the feet and fingers.

- **Dark skin patches (acanthosis nigricans):** Some people with type 2 diabetes may have far above normal levels of insulin in their blood, as their body is unable to utilize it due to insulin resistance. This increase of insulin in the bloodstream can lead to some skin cells over reproducing and cause dark patches to form on the skin.

Complications

Severe complications of diabetes can be debilitating and deadly. Both type 1 and type 2 diabetes can lead to serious neurological, cardiovascular, and optical conditions. Some of the most common complications of advanced diabetes are as follows:

•   **Heart attacks:** Diabetes is directly linked to a higher rate of heart attacks in adults. High blood glucose levels damage the cells and nerves around the heart and blood vessels over time, which can cause a plethora of heart diseases to form.

•   **Cataracts:** People with diabetes have a nearly 60 percent greater chance of developing cataracts later in life if their diabetes is left unchecked (Diabetes.co.uk, 2019a). Doctors are unsure of the exact reason for cataracts forming at a higher rate in diabetes patients, but many believe it has to do with the lower amounts of glucose available to the cells powering our eyes.

- **Peripheral artery disease (PAD):** This is a very common diabetes and This causes decreased blood flow, which leads to serious issues in the lower legs, often resulting in amputation.
- **Diabetic nephropathy:** Diabetic nephropathy happens when high levels of blood glucose damage parts of your kidneys, which is responsible for filtering blood. This causes your kidneys to develop chronic kidney diseases and break down over time, leading to failure.
- **Glaucoma:** Diabetes can cause glaucoma in sufferers due to high blood sugar levels and this directly damages blood vessels in the eyes. When your body attempts to repair these vessels, it may cause glaucoma on the iris where the damage was caused.

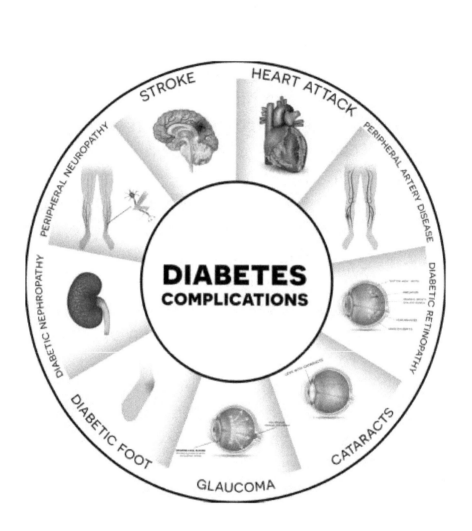

Treatment

Treatments for diabetes vary depending on the type, number, and severity of complications and health of the patient overall. Luckily, diabetes has been long studied by the medical community and, therefore, there is an abundance of resources and treatments available.

For type 1 diabetes, insulin supplements are essential. Type 1 diabetics rely on daily insulin injections; some prefer a costlier but easier-to-use insulin pump. Insulin needs in type 1 diabetics will vary throughout the day as they eat and exercise. This means many type 1 diabetics will regularly test their blood sugar levels to assess whether their insulin needs are being met.

Some type 1 diabetics develop insulin resistance after years of injections. This means that oral diabetes medication such as metformin is becoming increasingly more commonly prescribed to type 1 diabetics to help prevent insulin resistance.

Type 2 diabetes can be controlled without medication in some cases. Many type 2 diabetics can self-regulate their blood sugar levels through careful eating and light exercise. Most type 2 diabetics are recommended to stay on low-fat diets, which are high in fiber and healthy carbs.

Some type 2 diabetics do need medication. Unlike type 1, insulin is not nearly as commonly needed for type 2. But, some type 2 diabetics do need insulin to supplement the reduced amount their pancreas may provide.

The most common medication given to type 2 diabetics is metformin. This prescription drug helps lower blood glucose levels and improve insulin sensitivity. Other drugs prescribed to type 2 diabetics include sulfonylureas, thiazolidinediones, and meglitinides, which all help increase insulin production or sensitivity.

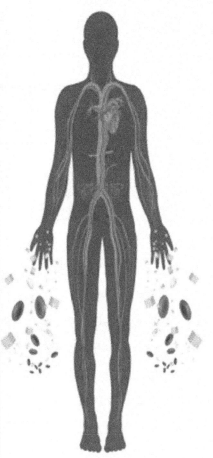

Diabetes
Blood Sugar Level

	HBA-1C Test Score	Mean Blood mg/dl	Glucose mmol/l
	14.0	380	21.1
	13.0	350	19.3
Action Suggested	12.0	315	17.4
	11.0	280	15.6
	10.0	250	13.7
	9.0	215	11.9
	8.0	180	10.0
Good	7.0	150	8.2
	6.0	115	6.3
Excellent	5.0	80	4.7
	4.0	50	2.6
	3.0	35	2.0

- Very high
- A little high to very high depending on patient
- Maximum after meal in nondiabetics
- Normal before meal in nondiabetics
- Normal
- Low
- Extremely low

" The normal range of blood sugar according to the glucose levels chart is between 70 and 100 mg/dl "

10 Tips to Control Diabetes

- **Eat less salt:** Salt can increase your chances of having high blood pressure, which leads to increased chances of heart disease and stroke.
- **Replace sugar:** Replace sugar with zero calorie sweeteners. Cutting out sugar gives you much more control over your blood sugar levels.
- **Cut out alcohol:** Alcohol tends to be high in calories, and if drunk on an empty stomach with insulin medication, it can cause drastic drops in blood sugar.
- **Be physically active:** Physical activity lowers your risk of cardiovascular issues and increases your body's natural glucose burn rate.
- **Avoid saturated fats:** Saturated fats like butter and pastries can lead to high cholesterol and blood circulation issues.
- **Use canola or olive oil:** If you need to use oil in your cooking, use canola or olive oil. Both are high in beneficial fatty acids and monounsaturated fat.

- **Drink water:** Water is by far the healthiest drink you can have. Drinking water helps to regulate blood sugar and insulin levels.

- **Make sure you get enough vitamin D:** Vitamin D is a crucial vitamin for controlling blood sugar levels. Eat food high in this vitamin or ask your doctor about supplements.

- **Avoid processed food:** Processed foods tend to be high in vegetable oils, salt, refined grains, or other unhealthy additives.

- **Drink coffee and tea:** Not only are coffee and tea great hunger suppressants for dieters, but they contain important antioxidants that help with protecting cells.

Ham and Egg Cups

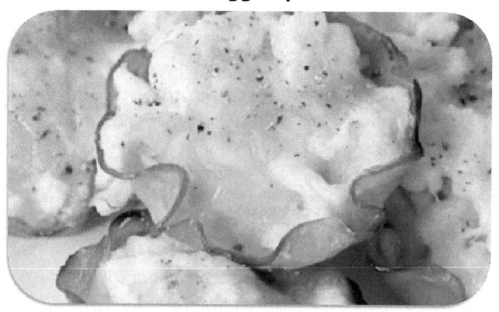

Preparation Time: 10 Minutes
Cooking Time: 15 Minutes
Servings: 4
Ingredients

- 5 slices ham
- 4 tbsp. cheese
- 1,5 tbsp. cream
- 3 egg whites
- 1,5 tbsp. pepper (green)
- 1 tsp. salt
- pepper to taste

Directions

1. Preheat oven to 350 F.
2. Arrange each slice of thinly sliced ham into 4 muffin tin.
3. Put 1/4 of grated cheese into ham cup.
4. Mix eggs, cream, salt and pepper and divide it into 2 tins.
5. Bake in oven 15 Minutes; after baking, sprinkle with green onions.

If you want to keep your current shape, also pay attention to this dish.

Nutrition:

Calories 180 / Protein 13 g / Fat 13 g / Carbs 2 g

Cauliflower Rice with Chicken

Preparation Time: 15 Minutes

Cooking Time: 15 Minutes

Servings: 4

Ingredients

- 1/2 large cauliflower
- 3/4 cup cooked meat
- 1/2 bell pepper
- 1 carrot
- 2 ribs celery
- 1 tbsp. stir fry sauce (low carb)
- 1 tbsp. extra virgin olive oil
- Salt and pepper to taste

Directions

1. Chop cauliflower in a processor to "rice." Place in a bowl.
2. Properly chop all vegetables in a food processor into thin slices.
3. Add cauliflower and other plants to WOK with heated oil. Fry until all veggies are tender.
4. Add chopped meat and sauce to the wok and fry 10 Minutes.

Serve.

This dish is very mouth-watering!

Nutrition:

Calories 200 / Protein 10 g / Fat 12 g /Carbs 10 g

Turkey with Fried Eggs

Preparation Time: 10 Minutes
Cooking Time: 20 Minutes
Servings: 4
Ingredients

- 4 large potatoes
- 1 cooked turkey thigh
- 1 large onion (about 2 cups diced)
- butter
- Chile flakes
- 4 eggs
- salt to taste
- pepper to taste

Directions

1. Rub the cold boiled potatoes on the coarsest holes of a box grater. Dice the turkey.
2. Cook the onion in as much unsalted butter as you feel comfortable with until it's just fragrant and translucent.
3. Add the rubbed potatoes and a cup of diced cooked turkey, salt and pepper to taste, and cook 20 Minutes.

Top each with a fried egg. Yummy!

Nutrition:

Calories 170 / Protein 19 g / Fat 7 g / Carbs 6 g

Sweet Potato, Kale, and White Bean Stew

Preparation time: 15 minutes
Cooking time: 25 minutes
Servings: 4
Ingredients:

- 1 (15-ounce) can low-sodium cannellini beans, rinsed and drained, divided

- 1 tablespoon olive oil

- 1 medium onion, chopped

- 2 garlic cloves, minced

- 2 celery stalks, chopped

- 3 medium carrots, chopped

- 2 cups low-sodium vegetable broth

- 1 teaspoon apple cider vinegar

- 2 medium sweet potatoes (about 1¼ pounds)

- 2 cups chopped kale

- 1 cup shelled edamame

- ¼ cup quinoa

- 1 teaspoon dried thyme

- 1/2 teaspoon cayenne pepper

- 1/2 teaspoon salt

- ¼ teaspoon freshly ground black pepper

Directions:

1. Put half the beans into a blender and blend until smooth. Set aside.

2. In a large soup pot over medium heat, heat the oil. When the oil is shining, include the onion and garlic, and cook until the onion softens and the garlic is sweet, about 3 minutes. Add the celery and carrots, and continue cooking until the vegetables soften, about 5 minutes.

3. Add the broth, vinegar, sweet potatoes, unblended beans, kale, edamame, and quinoa, and bring the mixture to a boil. Reduce the heat and simmer until the vegetables soften, about 10 minutes.

4. Add the blended beans, thyme, cayenne, salt, and black pepper, increase the heat to medium-high, and bring the mixture to a boil. Reduce the heat and simmer, uncovered, until the flavors combine, about 5 minutes.

5. Into each of 4 containers, scoop 1¾ cups of stew.

Nutrition: calories: 373; total fat: 7g; saturated fat: 1g; protein: 15g; total carbs: 65g; fiber: 15g; sugar: 13g; sodium: 540mg

Slow Cooker Two-Bean Sloppy Joes

Preparation time: 10 minutes
Cooking time: 6 hours
Servings: 4
Ingredients:

- 1 (15-ounce) can low-sodium black beans

- 1 (15-ounce) can low-sodium pinto beans

- 1 (15-ounce) can no-salt-added diced tomatoes

- 1 medium green bell pepper, cored, seeded, and chopped

- 1 medium yellow onion, chopped

- ¼ cup low-sodium vegetable broth

- 2 garlic cloves, minced

- 2 servings (¼ cup) meal prep barbecue sauce or bottled barbecue sauce

- ¼ teaspoon salt

- ¼ teaspoon freshly ground black pepper

- 4 whole-wheat buns

Directions:

1. In a slow cooker, combine the black beans, pinto beans, diced tomatoes, bell pepper, onion, broth, garlic, meal prep barbecue sauce, salt, and black pepper. Stir the ingredients, then cover and cook on low for 6 hours.

2. Into each of 4 containers, spoon 1¼ cups of sloppy joe mix. Serve with 1 whole-wheat bun.

3. Storage: place airtight containers in the refrigerator for up to 1 week. To freeze, place freezer-safe containers in the freezer for up to 2 months. To defrost, refrigerate overnight. To reheat individual portions, microwave uncovered on high for 2 to 21/2 minutes. Alternatively, reheat the entire dish in a saucepan on the stove top. Bring the sloppy joes to a boil, then reduce the heat and simmer until heated through, 10 to 15 minutes. Serve with a whole-wheat bun.

Nutrition: calories: 392; total fat: 3g; saturated fat: 0g; protein: 17g; total carbs: 79g; fiber: 19g; sugar: 15g; sodium: 759mg

Lighter Eggplant Parmesan

Preparation time: 15 minutes
Cooking time: 35 minutes
Servings: 4
Ingredients:

- Nonstick cooking spray

- 3 eggs, beaten

- 1 tablespoon dried parsley

- 2 teaspoons ground oregano

- 1/8 teaspoon freshly ground black pepper

- 1 cup panko bread crumbs, preferably whole-wheat

- 1 large eggplant (about 2 pounds)

- 5 servings (21/2 cups) chunky tomato sauce or jarred low-sodium tomato sauce

- 1 cup part-skim mozzarella cheese

- ¼ cup grated parmesan cheese

Directions:

1. Preheat the oven to 450f. Coat a baking sheet with cooking spray.

2. In a medium bowl, whisk together the eggs, parsley, oregano, and pepper.

3. Pour the panko into a separate medium bowl.

4. Slice the eggplant into ¼-inch-thick slices. Dip each slice of eggplant into the egg mixture, shaking off the excess. Then dredge both sides of the eggplant in the panko bread crumbs. Place the coated eggplant on the prepared baking sheet, leaving a 1/2-inch space between each slice.

5. Bake for about 15 minutes until soft and golden brown. Remove from the oven and set aside to slightly cool.

6. Pour 1/2 cup of chunky tomato sauce on the bottom of an 8-by-15-inch baking dish. Using a spatula or the back of a spoon spread the tomato sauce evenly. Place half the slices of cooked eggplant, slightly overlapping, in the dish, and top with 1 cup of chunky tomato sauce, 1/2 cup of mozzarella and 2 tablespoons of

grated parmesan. Repeat the layer, ending with the cheese.

7. Bake uncovered for 20 minutes until the cheese is bubbling and slightly browned.

8. Remove from the oven and allow cooling for 15 minutes before dividing the eggplant equally into 4 separate containers.

Nutrition: calories: 333; total fat: 14g; saturated fat: 6g; protein: 20g; total carbs: 35g; fiber: 11g; sugar: 15g; sodium: 994mg

Coconut-Lentil Curry

Preparation time: 15 minutes
Cooking time: 35 minutes
Servings: 4
Ingredients:

- 1 tablespoon olive oil

- 1 medium yellow onion, chopped

- 1 garlic clove, minced

- 1 medium red bell pepper, diced

- 1 (15-ounce) can green or brown lentils, rinsed and drained

- 2 medium sweet potatoes, washed, peeled, and cut into bite-size chunks (about 1¼ pounds)

- 1 (15-ounce) can no-salt-added diced tomatoes

- 2 tablespoons tomato paste

- 4 teaspoons curry powder

- 1/8 teaspoon ground cloves

- 1 (15-ounce) can light coconut milk

- ¼ teaspoon salt

- 2 pieces whole-wheat naan bread, halved, or 4 slices crusty bread

Directions:

1. In a large saucepan over medium heat, heat the olive oil. When the oil is shimmering, add both the onion and garlic and cook until the onion softens and the garlic is sweet, for about 3 minutes.

2. Add the bell pepper and continue cooking until it softens, about 5 minutes more. Add the lentils, sweet potatoes, tomatoes, tomato paste, curry powder, and cloves, and bring the mixture to a boil. Reduce the heat to medium-low, cover, and simmer until the potatoes are softened, about 20 minutes.

3. Add the coconut milk and salt, and return to a boil. Reduce the heat and simmer until the flavors combine, about 5 minutes.

4. Into each of 4 containers, spoon 2 cups of curry.

5. Enjoy each serving with half of a piece of naan bread or 1 slice of crusty bread.

Nutrition: calories: 559; total fat: 16g; saturated fat: 7g; protein: 16g; total carbs: 86g; fiber: 16g; sugar: 18g; sodium: 819mg

Stuffed Portobello with Cheese

Preparation time: 15 minutes
Cooking time: 25 minutes
Servings: 4
Ingredients:

- 4 Portobello mushroom caps

- 1 tablespoon olive oil

- 1/2 teaspoon salt, divided

- ¼ teaspoon freshly ground black pepper, divided

- 1 cup baby spinach, chopped

- 11/2 cups part-skim ricotta cheese

- 1/2 cup part-skim shredded mozzarella cheese

- ¼ cup grated parmesan cheese

- 1 garlic clove, minced

- 1 tablespoon dried parsley

- 2 teaspoons dried oregano

- 4 teaspoons unseasoned bread crumbs, divided

- 4 servings (4 cups) roasted broccoli with shallots

Directions:

1. Preheat the oven to 375f. Line a baking sheet with aluminum foil.

2. Brush the mushroom caps with the olive oil, and sprinkle with ¼ teaspoon salt and 1/8 teaspoon pepper. Put the mushroom caps on the prepared baking sheet and bake until soft, about 12 minutes.

3. In a medium bowl, mix together the spinach, ricotta, mozzarella, parmesan, garlic, parsley, oregano, and the remaining ¼ teaspoon of salt and 1/8 teaspoon of pepper.

4. Spoon 1/2 cup of cheese mixture into each mushroom cap, and sprinkle each with 1 teaspoon of bread crumbs. Return the mushrooms to the oven for an additional 8 to 10 minutes until warmed through.

5. Remove from the oven and allow the mushrooms to cool for about 10

minutes before placing each in an individual container. Add 1 cup of roasted broccoli with shallots to each container.

Nutrition: calories: 419; total fat: 30g; saturated fat: 10g; protein: 23g; total carbs: 19g; fiber: 2g; sugar: 3g; sodium: 790mg

Lighter Shrimp Scampi

Preparation time: 15 minutes
Cooking time: 15 minutes
Servings: 4
Ingredients:

- 11/2 pounds large peeled and deveined shrimp

- ¼ teaspoon salt

- 1/8 teaspoon freshly ground black pepper

- 2 tablespoons olive oil

- 1 shallot, chopped

- 2 garlic cloves, minced

- ¼ cup cooking white wine

- Juice of 1/2 lemon (1 tablespoon)

- 1/2 teaspoon sriracha

- 2 tablespoons unsalted butter, at room temperature

- ¼ cup chopped fresh parsley

- 4 servings (6 cups) zucchini noodles with lemon vinaigrette

Directions:

1. Season the shrimp with the salt and pepper.

2. In a medium saucepan over medium heat, heat the oil. Add the shallot and garlic, and cook until the shallot softens and the garlic is fragrant, about 3 minutes. Add the shrimp, cover, and cook until opaque, 2 to 3 minutes on each side. Using a slotted spoon, transfer the shrimp to a large plate.

3. Add the wine, lemon juice, and sriracha to the saucepan, and stir to combine. Bring the mixture to a boil, then reduce the heat and simmer until the liquid is reduced by about half, 3 minutes. Add the butter and stir until melted, about 3 minutes. Return the shrimp to the saucepan and toss to coat. Add the parsley and stir to combine.

4. Into each of 4 containers, place 11/2 cups of zucchini noodles with lemon

vinaigrette, and top with ¾ cup of scampi.

Nutrition: calories: 364; total fat: 21g; saturated fat: 6g; protein: 37g; total carbs: 10g; fiber: 2g; sugar: 6g; sodium: 557mg

Maple-Mustard Salmon

Preparation time: 10 minutes, plus 30 minutes marinating time
Cooking time: 20 minutes
Servings: 4
Ingredients:

- Nonstick cooking spray

- 1/2 cup 100% maple syrup

- 2 tablespoons Dijon mustard

- ¼ teaspoon salt

- 4 (5-ounce) salmon fillets

- 4 servings (4 cups) roasted broccoli with shallots

- 4 servings (2 cups) parsleyed whole-wheat couscous

Directions:

1. Preheat the oven to 400f. Line a baking sheet with aluminum foil and coat with cooking spray.

2. In a medium bowl, whisk together the maple syrup, mustard, and salt until smooth.

3. Put the salmon fillets into the bowl and toss to coat. Cover and place in the refrigerator to marinate for at least 30 minutes and up to overnight.

4. Shake off excess marinade from the salmon fillets and place them on the prepared baking sheet, leaving a 1-inch space between each fillet. Discard the extra marinade.

5. Bake for about 20 minutes until the salmon is opaque and a thermometer inserted in the thickest part of a fillet reads 145f.

6. Into each of 4 resealable containers, place 1 salmon fillet, 1 cup of roasted broccoli with shallots, and 1/2 cup of parsleyed whole-wheat couscous.

Nutrition: calories: 601; total fat: 29g; saturated fat: 4g; protein: 36g; total carbs: 51g; fiber: 3g; sugar: 23g; sodium: 610mg

Chicken Salad with Grapes and Pecans

Preparation Time: 15 Minutes
Cooking Time: 5 Minutes
Servings: 4
Ingredients:

- 1/3 cup unsalted pecans, chopped

- 10 ounces cooked skinless, boneless chicken breast or rotisserie chicken, finely chopped

- 1/2 medium yellow onion, finely chopped

- 1 celery stalk, finely chopped

- ¾ cup red or green seedless grapes, halved

- ¼ cup light mayonnaise

- ¼ cup nonfat plain Greek yogurt

- 1 tablespoon Dijon mustard

- 1 tablespoon dried parsley

- ¼ teaspoon salt

- 1/8 teaspoon freshly ground black pepper

- 1 cup shredded romaine lettuce

- 4 (8-inch) whole-wheat pitas

Directions:

1. Heat a small skillet over medium-low heat to toast the pecans. Cook the pecans until fragrant, about 3 minutes. Remove from the heat and set aside to cool.

2. In a medium bowl, mix the chicken, onion, celery, pecans, and grapes.

3. In a small bowl, whisk together the mayonnaise, yogurt, mustard, parsley, salt, and pepper. Spoon the sauce over the chicken mixture and stir until well combined.

4. Into each of 4 containers, place ¼ cup of lettuce and top with 1 cup of chicken salad. Store the pitas separately until ready to serve.

5. When ready to eat, stuff the serving of salad and lettuce into 1 pita.

Nutrition: Calories: 418; Total Fat: 14g; Saturated Fat: 2g; Protein: 31g; Total Carbs: 43g; Fiber: 6g;

Roasted Vegetables

Preparation time: 14 minutes
Cooking time: 17 minutes
Servings: 3
Ingredients:

- 4 Tbsp. olive oil, reserve some for greasing

- 2 heads, large garlic, tops sliced off

- 2 large eggplants/aubergine, tops removed, cubed

- 2 large shallots, peeled, quartered

- 1 large carrot, peeled, cubed

- 1 large parsnips, peeled, cubed

- 1 small green bell pepper, deseeded, ribbed, cubed

- 1 small red bell pepper, deseeded, ribbed, cubed

- ½ pound Brussels sprouts, halved, do not remove cores

- 1 sprig, large thyme, leaves picked

- sea salt, coarse-grained

For garnish
- 1 large lemon, halved, ½ squeezed, ½ sliced into smaller wedges

- ⅛ cup fennel bulb, minced

Directions:

1. From 425°F or 220°C preheat oven for at least 5 minutes before using.

2. Line deep roasting pan with aluminum foil; lightly grease with oil. Tumble in bell peppers, Brussels sprouts, carrots, eggplants, garlic, parsnips, rosemary leaves, shallots, and thyme. Add a pinch of sea salt; drizzle in remaining oil and lemon juice. Toss well to combine.

3. Cover roasting pan with a sheet of aluminum foil. Place this on middle rack of oven. Bake for 20 to 30 minutes. Remove aluminum foil. Roast, for another 5 to 10 minutes, or until some vegetables brown at the edges. Remove roasting pan from oven. Cool slightly before ladling equal portions into plates.

4. Garnish with fennel and a wedge of lemon. Squeeze lemon juice on top of dish before eating.

Nutrition:

Calories 163

Total Fat 4.2 g

Saturated Fat 0.8 g

Cholesterol 0 mg

Sodium 861 mg

Total Carbs 22.5 g

Fiber 6.3 g

Sugar 2.3 g

Protein 9.2 g

Millet Pilaf

Preparation time: 10 minutes
Cooking time: 15 minutes
Servings: 4
Ingredients:

- 1 cup millet
- 2 tomatoes, rinsed, seeded, and chopped
- 1¾ cups filtered water
- 2 tablespoons extra-virgin olive oil
- ¼ cup chopped dried apricot
- Zest of 1 lemon
- Juice of 1 lemon
- ½ cup fresh parsley, rinsed and chopped
- Himalayan pink salt
- Freshly ground black pepper

Directions:

1. In an electric pressure cooker, combine the millet, tomatoes, and water. Lock the lid into place, select Manual and High Pressure, and cook for 7 minutes.

2. When the beep sounds, quick release the pressure by pressing Cancel and twisting the steam valve to the Venting position. Carefully remove the lid.

3. Stir in the olive oil, apricot, lemon zest, lemon juice, and parsley. Taste, season with salt and pepper, and serve.

Nutrition:
Calories: 270
Total fat: 8g
Total carbohydrates: 42g
Fiber: 5g
Sugar: 3g
Protein: 6g

Sweet and Sour Onions

Preparation time: 10 minutes
Cooking time: 11 minutes
Servings: 4
Ingredients:

- 4 large onions, halved

- 2 garlic cloves, crushed

- 3 cups vegetable stock

- 1 ½ tablespoon balsamic vinegar

- ½ teaspoon Dijon mustard

- 1 tablespoon sugar

Directions:

1. Combine onions and garlic in a pan. Fry for 3 minutes, or till softened.

2. Pour stock, vinegar, Dijon mustard, and sugar. Bring to a boil.

3. Reduce heat. Cover and let the combination simmer for 10 minutes.

4. Get rid of from heat. Continue stirring until the liquid is reduced and the onions are brown. Serve.

Nutrition:

Calories 203
Total Fat 41.2 g
Saturated Fat 0.8 g
Cholesterol 0 mg
Sodium 861 mg
Total Carbs 29.5 g
Fiber 16.3 g
Sugar 29.3 g
Protein 19.2 g

Sautéed Apples and Onions

Preparation time: 14 minutes
Cooking time: 16 minutes
Servings: 3
Ingredients:

- 2 cups dry cider

- 1 large onion, halved

- 2 cups vegetable stock

- 4 apples, sliced into wedges

- Pinch of salt

- Pinch of pepper

Directions:

1. Combine cider and onion in a saucepan. Bring to a boil until the onions are cooked and liquid almost gone.

2. Pour the stock and the apples. Season with salt and pepper. Stir occasionally. Cook for about 10 minutes or until the apples are tender but not mushy. Serve.

Nutrition:
Calories 343
Total Fat 51.2 g
Saturated Fat 0.8 g
Cholesterol 0 mg
Sodium 861 mg
Total Carbs 22.5 g
Fiber 6.3 g
Sugar 2.3 g
Protein 9.2 g

Zucchini Noodles with Portabella Mushrooms

Preparation time: 14 minutes
Cooking time: 16 minutes
Servings: 3
Ingredients:

- 1 zucchini, processed into spaghetti-like noodles

- 3 garlic cloves, minced

- 2 white onions, thinly sliced

- 1 thumb-sized ginger, julienned

- 1 lb. chicken thighs

- 1 lb. portabella mushrooms, sliced into thick slivers

- 2 cups chicken stock

- 3 cups water

- Pinch of sea salt, add more if needed

- Pinch of black pepper, add more if needed

- 2 tsp. sesame oil

- 4 Tbsp. coconut oil, divided

- ¼ cup fresh chives, minced, for garnish

Directions:

1. Pour 2 tablespoons of coconut oil into a large saucepan. Fry mushroom slivers in batches for 5 minutes or until seared brown. Set aside. Transfer these to a plate.

2. Sauté the onion, garlic, and ginger for 3 minutes or until tender. Add in chicken thighs, cooked mushrooms, chicken stock, water, salt, and pepper stir mixture well. Bring to a boil.

3. Decrease gradually the heat and allow simmering for 20 minutes or until the chicken is forking tender. Tip in sesame oil.

4. Serve by placing an equal amount of zucchini noodles into bowls. Ladle soup and garnish with chives.

Nutrition:

Calories 163

Total Fat 4.2 g

Saturated Fat 0.8 g

Cholesterol 0 mg

Sodium 861 mg

Total Carbs 22.5 g

Fiber 6.3 g

Sugar 2.3 g

Protein 9.2 g

Grilled Tempeh with Pineapple

Preparation time: 12 minutes
Cooking time: 16 minutes
Servings: 3
Ingredients:

- 10 oz. tempeh, sliced

- 1 red bell pepper, quartered

- 1/4 pineapple, sliced into rings

- 6 oz. green beans

- 1 tbsp. coconut aminos

- 2 1/2 tbsp. orange juice, freshly squeeze

- 1 1/2 tbsp. lemon juice, freshly squeezed

- 1 tbsp. extra virgin olive oil

- 1/4 cup hoisin sauce

Directions:

1. Blend together the olive oil, orange and lemon juices, coconut aminos or soy sauce, and hoisin sauce in a bowl. Add the diced tempeh and set aside.

2. Heat up the grill or place a grill pan over medium high flame. Once hot, lift the marinated tempeh from the bowl with a pair of tongs and transfer them to the grill or pan.

3. Grille for 2 to 3 minutes, or until browned all over.

4. Grill the sliced pineapples alongside the tempeh, then transfer them directly onto the serving platter.

5. Place the grilled tempeh beside the grilled pineapple and cover with aluminum foil to keep warm.

6. Meanwhile, place the green beans and bell peppers in a bowl and add just enough of the marinade to coat.

7. Prepare the grill pan and add the vegetables. Grill until fork tender and slightly charred.

8. Transfer the grilled vegetables to the serving platter and arrange artfully with the tempeh and pineapple. Serve at once.

Nutrition:

Calories 163

Total Fat 4.2 g

Saturated Fat 0.8 g

Cholesterol 0 mg

Sodium 861 mg

Total Carbs 22.5 g

Fiber 6.3 g

Sugar 2.3 g

Protein 9.2 g

Courgettes In Cider Sauce

Preparation time: 13 minutes
Cooking time: 17 minutes
Servings: 3
Ingredients:

- 2 cups baby courgettes

- 3 tablespoons vegetable stock

- 2 tablespoons apple cider vinegar

- 1 tablespoon light brown sugar

- 4 spring onions, finely sliced

- 1 piece fresh gingerroot, grated

- 1 teaspoon corn flour

- 2 teaspoons water

Directions:

1. Bring a pan with salted water to a boil. Add courgettes. Bring to a boil for 5 minutes.

2. Meanwhile, in a pan, combine vegetable stock, apple cider vinegar, brown sugar, onions, gingerroot, lemon juice and rind, and orange juice and rind. Take to a boil. Lower the

heat and allow simmering for 3 minutes.

3. Mix the corn flour with water. Stir well. Pour into the sauce. Continue stirring until the sauce thickens.

4. Drain courgettes. Transfer to the serving dish. Spoon over the sauce. Toss to coat courgettes. Serve.

Nutrition:

Calories 173

Total Fat 9.2 g

Saturated Fat 0.8 g

Cholesterol 0 mg

Sodium 861 mg

Total Carbs 22.5 g

Fiber 6.3 g

Sugar 2.3 g

Protein 9.2 g

Baked Mixed Mushrooms

Preparation time: 8 minutes
Cooking time: 20 minutes
Servings: 3
Ingredients:
- 2 cups mixed wild mushrooms
- 1 cup chestnut mushrooms
- 2 cups dried porcini
- 2 shallots
- 4 garlic cloves
- 3 cups raw pecans
- ½ bunch fresh thyme
- 1 bunch flat-leaf parsley
- 2 tablespoons olive oil
- 2 fresh bay leaves
- 1 ½ cups stale bread

Directions:
1. Remove skin and finely chop garlic and shallots. Roughly chop the wild mushrooms and chestnut mushrooms. Pick the leaves of the thyme and tear

---

the bread into small pieces. Put inside the pressure cooker.

2. Place the pecans and roughly chop the nuts. Pick the parsley leaves and roughly chop.

3. Place the porcini in a bowl then add 300ml of boiling water. Set aside until needed.

4. Heat oil in the pressure cooker. Add the garlic and shallots. Cook for 3 minutes while stirring occasionally.

5. Drain porcini and reserve the liquid. Add the porcini into the pressure cooker together with the wild mushrooms and chestnut mushrooms. Add the bay leaves and thyme.

6. Position the lid and lock in place. Put to high heat and bring to high pressure. Adjust heat to stabilize. Cook for 10 minutes. Adjust taste if necessary.

7. Transfer the mushroom mixture into a bowl and set aside to cool completely.

8. Once the mushrooms are completely cool, add the bread, pecans, a pinch of black pepper and sea salt, and half of the reserved liquid into the bowl. Mix well. Add more reserved liquid if the mixture seems dry.

9. Add more than half of the parsley into the bowl and stir. Transfer the mixture into a 20cm x 25cm lightly greased baking dish and cover with tin foil.

10.   Bake in the oven for 35 minutes. Then, get rid of the foil and cook for another 10 minutes. Once done, sprinkle the remaining parsley on top and serve with bread or crackers. Serve.

Nutrition:

Calories 343

Total Fat 4.2 g

Saturated Fat 0.8 g

Cholesterol 0 mg

Sodium 861 mg

Total Carbs 22.5 g

Fiber 6.3 g

Sugar 2.3 g

Protein 9.2 g

Spiced Okra

Preparation time: 14 minutes
Cooking time: 16 minutes
Servings: 3
Ingredients:

- 2 cups okra

- ¼ teaspoon stevia

- 1 teaspoon chilli powder

- ½ teaspoon ground turmeric

- 1 tablespoon ground coriander

- 2 tablespoons fresh coriander, chopped

- 1 tablespoon ground cumin

- ¼ teaspoon salt

- 1 tablespoon desiccated coconut

- 3 tablespoons vegetable oil

- ½ teaspoon black mustard seeds

- ½ teaspoon cumin seeds

- Fresh tomatoes, to garnish

Directions:
1. Trim okra. Wash and dry.

2. Combine stevia, chilli powder, turmeric, ground coriander, fresh coriander, cumin, salt, and desiccated coconut in a bowl.

3. Heat the oil in a pan. Cook mustard and cumin seeds for 3 minutes. Stir continuously. Add okra. Tip in the spice mixture. Cook on low heat for 8 minutes.

4. Transfer to a serving dish. Garnish with fresh tomatoes.

Nutrition:
Calories 163
Total Fat 4.2 g
Saturated Fat 0.8 g
Cholesterol 0 mg
Sodium 861 mg
Total Carbs 22.5 g
Fiber 6.3 g
Sugar 2.3 g
Protein 9.2 g

Dinner Recipes

Misto Quente

Preparation time: 5 minutes

Cooking time: 10 minutes

Servings: 4

Ingredients:

- 4 slices of bread without shell
- 4 slices of turkey breast
- 4 slices of cheese
- 2 tbsp. cream cheese
- 2 spoons of butter

Directions:

1. Preheat the air fryer. Set the timer of 5 minutes and the temperature to 200C.
2. Pass the butter on one side of the slice of bread, and on the other side of the slice, the cream cheese.
3. Mount the sandwiches placing two slices of turkey breast and two slices cheese between the breads, with the cream cheese inside and the side with butter.
4. Place the sandwiches in the basket of the air fryer. Set the timer of the air fryer for 5 minutes and press the power button.

Nutrition: Calories: 340 Fat: 15g
Carbohydrates: 32g Protein: 15g Sugar: 0g
Cholesterol: 0mg

Garlic Bread

Preparation time: 10 minutes

Cooking time: 15 minutes

Servings: 4-5

Ingredients:

- 2 stale French rolls
- 4 tbsp. crushed or crumpled garlic
- 1 cup of mayonnaise
- Powdered grated Parmesan
- 1 tbsp. olive oil

Directions:

1. Preheat the air fryer. Set the time of 5 minutes and the temperature to 2000C.
2. Mix mayonnaise with garlic and set aside.
3. Cut the baguettes into slices, but without separating them completely.
4. Fill the cavities of equals. Brush with olive oil and sprinkle with grated cheese.
5. Place in the basket of the air fryer. Set the timer to 10 minutes, adjust the temperature to 1800C and press the power button.

Nutrition: Calories: 340 Fat: 15g
Carbohydrates: 32g Protein: 15g Sugar: 0g
Cholesterol: 0mg

Bruschetta

Preparation time: 5 minutes

Cooking time: 10 minutes

Servings: 2

Ingredients:

- 4 slices of Italian bread
- 1 cup chopped tomato tea
- 1 cup grated mozzarella tea
- Olive oil
- Oregano, salt, and pepper
- 4 fresh basil leaves

Directions:

1. Preheat the air fryer. Set the timer of 5 minutes and the temperature to 2000C.
2. Sprinkle the slices of Italian bread with olive oil. Divide the chopped tomatoes and mozzarella between the slices. Season with salt, pepper, and oregano.
3. Put oil in the filling. Place a basil leaf on top of each slice.
4. Put the bruschetta in the basket of the air fryer being careful not to spill the filling. Set the timer of 5

minutes, set the temperature to 180C, and press the power button.

5. Transfer the bruschetta to a plate and serve.

Nutrition: Calories: 434 Fat: 14g Carbohydrates: 63g Protein: 11g Sugar: 8g Cholesterol: 0mg

Cream Buns with Strawberries

Preparation time: 10 minutes

Cooking time: 12 minutes

Servings: 6

Ingredients:

- 240g all-purpose flour
- 50g granulated sugar
- 8g baking powder
- 1g of salt
- 85g chopped cold butter
- 84g chopped fresh strawberries
- 120 ml whipping cream
- 2 large eggs
- 10 ml vanilla extract
- 5 ml of water

Directions:

1. Sift flour, sugar, baking powder and salt in a large bowl. Put the butter with the flour with the use of a blender or your hands until the mixture resembles thick crumbs.
2. Mix the strawberries in the flour mixture. Set aside for the mixture to stand. Beat the whipping cream, 1 egg and the vanilla extract in a separate bowl.

3. Put the cream mixture in the flour mixture until they are homogeneous, and then spread the mixture to a thickness of 38 mm.
4. Use a round cookie cutter to cut the buns. Spread the buns with a combination of egg and water. Set aside
5. Preheat the air fryer, set it to 180C.
6. Place baking paper in the preheated inner basket.
7. Place the buns on top of the baking paper and cook for 12 minutes at 180C, until golden brown.

Nutrition: Calories: 150Fat: 14g Carbohydrates: 3g Protein: 11g Sugar: 8g Cholesterol: 0mg

Blueberry Buns

Preparation time: 10 minutes

Cooking time: 12 minutes

Servings: 6

Ingredients:

- 240g all-purpose flour
- 50g granulated sugar
- 8g baking powder
- 2g of salt
- 85g chopped cold butter
- 85g of fresh blueberries
- 3g grated fresh ginger
- 113 ml whipping cream
- 2 large eggs
- 4 ml vanilla extract
- 5 ml of water

Directions:

1. Put sugar, flour, baking powder and salt in a large bowl.
2. Put the butter with the flour using a blender or your hands until the mixture resembles thick crumbs.
3. Mix the blueberries and ginger in the flour mixture and set aside

4. Mix the whipping cream, 1 egg and the vanilla extract in a different container.
5. Put the cream mixture with the flour mixture until combined.
6. Shape the dough until it reaches a thickness of approximately 38 mm and cut it into eighths.
7. Spread the buns with a combination of egg and water. Set aside Preheat the air fryer set it to 180C.
8. Place baking paper in the preheated inner basket and place the buns on top of the paper. Cook for 12 minutes at 180C, until golden brown

Nutrition: Calories: 105 Fat: 1.64g Carbohydrates: 20.09gProtein: 2.43g Sugar: 2.1g Cholesterol: 0mg

Cauliflower Potato Mash

Preparation Time: 30 minutes Servings: 4

Cooking Time: 5 minutes

Ingredients:

- 2 cups potatoes, peeled and cubed
- 2 tbsp. butter
- ¼ cup milk
- 10 oz. cauliflower florets
- ¾ tsp. salt

Directions:

1. Add water to the saucepan and bring to boil.
2. Reduce heat and simmer for 10 minutes.
3. Drain vegetables well. Transfer vegetables, butter, milk, and salt in a blender and blend until smooth.
4. Serve and enjoy.

Nutrition: Calories 128 Fat 6.2 g, Sugar 3.3 g, Protein 3.2 g, Cholesterol 17 mg

French toast in Sticks

Preparation time: 5 minutes

Cooking time: 10 minutes

Servings: 4

Ingredients:

- 4 slices of white bread, 38 mm thick, preferably hard
- 2 eggs
- 60 ml of milk
- 15 ml maple sauce
- 2 ml vanilla extract
- Nonstick Spray Oil
- 38g of sugar
- 3ground cinnamon
- Maple syrup, to serve
- Sugar to sprinkle

Directions:

1. Cut each slice of bread into thirds making 12 pieces. Place sideways
2. Beat the eggs, milk, maple syrup and vanilla.
3. Preheat the air fryer, set it to 175C.
4. Dip the sliced bread in the egg mixture and place it in the preheated air fryer. Sprinkle

French toast generously with oil spray.

5. Cook French toast for 10 minutes at 175C. Turn the toast halfway through cooking.
6. Mix the sugar and cinnamon in a bowl.
7. Cover the French toast with the sugar and cinnamon mixture when you have finished cooking.
8. Serve with Maple syrup and sprinkle with powdered sugar

Nutrition: Calories 128 Fat 6.2 g, Carbohydrates 16.3 g, Sugar 3.3 g, Protein 3.2 g, Cholesterol 17 mg

Muffins Sandwich

Preparation time: 2 minutes

Cooking time: 10 minutes

Servings: 1

Ingredients:

- Nonstick Spray Oil
- 1 slice of white cheddar cheese
- 1 slice of Canadian bacon
- 1 English muffin, divided
- 15 ml hot water
- 1 large egg
- Salt and pepper to taste

Directions:

1. Spray the inside of an 85g mold with oil spray and place it in the air fryer.
2. Preheat the air fryer, set it to 160C.
3. Add the Canadian cheese and bacon in the preheated air fryer.
4. Pour the hot water and the egg into the hot pan and season with salt and pepper.
5. Select Bread, set to 10 minutes.

6. Take out the English muffins after 7 minutes, leaving the egg for the full time.
7. Build your sandwich by placing the cooked egg on top of the English muffing and serve

Nutrition: Calories 400 Fat 26g, Carbohydrates 26g, Sugar 15 g, Protein 3 g, Cholesterol 155 mg

Bacon BBQ

Preparation time: 2 minutes

Cooking time: 8 minutes

Servings: 2

Ingredients:

- 13g dark brown sugar
- 5g chili powder
- 1g ground cumin
- 1g cayenne pepper
- 4 slices of bacon, cut in half

Directions:

1. Mix seasonings until well combined.
2. Dip the bacon in the dressing until it is completely covered. Leave aside.
3. Preheat the air fryer, set it to 160C.
4. Place the bacon in the preheated air fryer
5. Select Bacon and press Start/Pause.

Nutrition: Calories: 1124 Fat: 72g Carbohydrates: 59g Protein: 49g Sugar: 11g Cholesterol: 77mg

Stuffed French toast

Preparation time: 4 minutes

Cooking time: 10 minutes

Servings: 1

Ingredients:

- 1 slice of brioche bread,
- 64 mm thick, preferably rancid
- 113g cream cheese
- 2 eggs
- 15 ml of milk
- 30 ml whipping cream
- 38g of sugar
- 3g cinnamon
- 2 ml vanilla extract
- Nonstick Spray Oil
- Pistachios chopped to cover
- Maple syrup, to serve

Directions:

1. Preheat the air fryer, set it to 175C.
2. Cut a slit in the middle of the muffin.
3. Fill the inside of the slit with cream cheese. Leave aside.

4. Mix the eggs, milk, whipping cream, sugar, cinnamon, and vanilla extract.
5. Moisten the stuffed French toast in the egg mixture for 10 seconds on each side.
6. Sprinkle each side of French toast with oil spray.
7. Place the French toast in the preheated air fryer and cook for 10 minutes at 175C
8. Stir the French toast carefully with a spatula when you finish cooking.
9. Serve topped with chopped pistachios and acrid syrup.

Nutrition: Calories: 159Fat: 7.5g Carbohydrates: 25.2g Protein: 14g Sugar: 0g Cholesterol: 90mg

Scallion Sandwich

Preparation Time: 10 minutes

Cooking Time: 10 minutes

Servings: 1

Ingredients:

- 2 slices wheat bread
- 2 teaspoons butter, low fat
- 2 scallions, sliced thinly
- 1 tablespoon of parmesan cheese, grated
- 3/4 cup of cheddar cheese, reduced fat, grated

Directions:

1. Preheat the Air fryer to 356 degrees.
2. Spread butter on a slice of bread. Place inside the cooking basket with the butter side facing down.
3. Place cheese and scallions on top. Spread the rest of the butter on the other slice of bread Put it on top of the sandwich and sprinkle with parmesan cheese.
4. Cook for 10 minutes.

Nutrition: Calorie: 154Carbohydrate: 9g Fat: 2.5g Protein: 8.6g Fiber: 2.4g

Lean Lamb and Turkey Meatballs with Yogurt

Preparation Time: 10 minutes

Servings: 4

Cooking Time: 8 minutes

Ingredients:

- 1 egg white
- 4 ounces ground lean turkey
- 1 pound of ground lean lamb
- 1 teaspoon each of cayenne pepper, ground coriander, red chili pastes, salt, and ground cumin
- 2 garlic cloves, minced
- 1 1/2 tablespoons parsley, chopped
- 1 tablespoon mint, chopped
- 1/4 cup of olive oil

For the yogurt

- 2 tablespoons of buttermilk
- 1 garlic clove, minced
- 1/4 cup mint, chopped
- 1/2 cup of Greek yogurt, non-fat
- Salt to taste

Directions:

1. Set the Air Fryer to 390 degrees.

2. Mix all the ingredients for the meatballs in a bowl. Roll and mold them into golf-size round pieces. Arrange in the cooking basket. Cook for 8 minutes.
3. While waiting, combine all the ingredients for the mint yogurt in a bowl. Mix well.
4. Serve the meatballs with the mint yogurt. Top with olives and fresh mint.

5. Nutrition: Calorie: 154 Carbohydrate: 9g Fat: 2.5g Protein: 8.6g Fiber: 2.4g

Conclusion

I hope you have enjoyed these recipes as much as I have. Life with diabetes should not be hard. It is not the end—it is the beginning. With healthy dietary management, you can lead a life free from the negative effects of high (or low) blood sugar levels.

With the knowledge I have shared, you now know why you may have become diabetic, you know what this means, and now, you also know how to manage it. You are armed with resources, apps, and recipes to help you along this lifelong journey. Food is not your enemy; it's your friend.

Cook your way to health and vitality with these recipes and tips. Good things are made to share, so please help a friend find out about this way of life. Call them over for a meal, talk about diabetes, and let's help create awareness as we feast on every delectable spoonful of diabetic cooking made easy.

The warning symptoms of diabetes type 1 are the same as type 2, however, in type 1, these signs and symptoms tend to occur slowly over a period of months or years, making it harder to spot and recognize. Some of these symptoms can even occur after the disease has progressed.

Each disorder has risk factors that when found in an individual, favor the development of the disease. Diabetes is no different. Here are some of the risk factors for developing diabetes.

Having a Family History of Diabetes

Usually having a family member, especially first-degree relatives could be an indicator that you are at risk to develop diabetes. Your risk of developing diabetes is about 15% if you have one parent with diabetes while it is 75% if both your parents have diabetes.

Having Prediabetes

Being pre-diabetic means that you have higher than normal blood glucose levels. However, they are not high enough to be diagnosed as type 2 diabetes. Having pre-diabetes is a risk factor for developing type 2 diabetes as well as other conditions such as cardiac conditions. Since there are no symptoms or signs for prediabetes, it is often a latent condition that is discovered accidentally during routine investigations of blood glucose levels or when investigating other conditions.

Being Obese or Overweight

Your metabolism, fat stores and eating habits when you are overweight or above the healthy weight range contributes to abnormal metabolism pathways that put you at risk for developing diabetes type 2. There have been consistent research results of the obvious link between developing diabetes and being obese.

Having a Sedentary Lifestyle

Having a lifestyle where you are mostly physically inactive predisposes you to a lot of conditions including diabetes type 2. That is because being physically inactive causes you to develop obesity or become overweight. Moreover, you don't burn any excess sugars that you ingest which can lead you to become prediabetic and eventually diabetic.

Having Gestational Diabetes Developing gestational diabetes which is diabetes that occurred due to pregnancy (and often disappears after pregnancy) is a risk factor for developing diabetes at some point.

Ethnicity

Belonging to certain ethnic groups such as Middle Eastern, South Asian or Indian background. Studies of statistics have revealed that the prevalence of diabetes type 2 in these ethnic groups is high. If you come from any of these ethnicities, this puts you at risk of developing diabetes type 2 yourself.

Having Hypertension

Studies have shown an association between having hypertension and having an increased risk of developing diabetes. If you have hypertension, you should not leave it uncontrolled. Extremes of Age Diabetes can occur at any age. However, being too young or too old means your body is not in its best form and therefore, this increases the risk of developing diabetes. That sounds scary. However, diabetes only occurs with the presence of a combination of these risk factors. Most of the risk factors can be minimized by taking action. For example, developing a more active lifestyle, taking care of your habits and attempting to lower your blood glucose sugar by restricting your sugar intake. If you start to notice you are prediabetic or getting overweight, etc., there is always something you can do to modify the situation. Recent studies show that developing healthy eating habits and following diets that are low in carbs, losing excess weight and leading an active lifestyle can help to protect you from developing diabetes, especially diabetes type 2, by minimizing the risk factors of developing the disorder.

You can also have an oral glucose tolerance test in which you will have a fasting glucose test first and then you will be given a sugary drink and then having your blood glucose tested 2 hours after that to see how your body responds to glucose meals. In healthy individuals, the blood glucose should drop again 2 hours post sugary meals due to the action of insulin.

Another indicative test is the HbA1C. This test reflects the average of your blood glucose level over the last 2 to 3 months. It is also a test to see how well you manage your diabetes.

People with diabetes type 1 require compulsory insulin shots to control their diabetes because they have no other option. People with diabetes type 2 can regulate their diabetes with healthy eating and regular physical activity although they may require some glucose-lowering medications that can be in tablet form or in the form of an injection.

All the above goes in the direction that you need to avoid a starchy diet because of its tendency to raise the blood glucose levels. Too many carbohydrates can lead to insulin sensitivity and pancreatic fatigue; as well as weight gain with all its associated risk factors for cardiovascular disease and hypertension. The solution is to lower your sugar intake, therefore, decrease your body's need for insulin and increase the burning of fat in your body.

When your body is low on sugars, it will be forced to use a subsequent molecule to burn for energy, in that case, this will be fat. The burning of fat will lead you to lose weight.

I hope you have learned something!